Level A · Book 1

QuickReads®
A Research-Based Fluency Program

Elfrieda H. Hiebert, Ph.D.

MODERN CURRICULUM PRESS

Pearson Learning Group

Program Reviewers and Consultants

Dr. Barbara A. Baird
Director of Federal Programs/Richardson ISD
Richardson, TX

Dr. Kate Kinsella
Dept. of Secondary Education and Step to College Program
San Francisco State University
San Francisco, CA

Pat Sears
Early Child Coordinator/Virginia Beach Public Schools
Virginia Beach, VA

Dr. Judith B. Smith
Supervisor of ESOL and World and Classical Languages/Baltimore City Public Schools
Baltimore, MD

The following people have contributed to the development of this product:

Art and Design: Denise Ingrassia, David Mager, Judy Mahoney,
   Salita Mehta, Elbaliz Mendez, Dan Thomas, Dan Trush

Editorial: Lynn W. Kloss

Inventory: Levon Carter

Marketing: Alison Bruno

Production/Manufacturing: Lorraine Allen, Carlos Blas, Leslie Greenberg

Publishing Operations: Jennifer Van Der Heide

1-800-321-3106
www.pearsonlearning.com

Contents

Contents

SCIENCE **Your Five Senses**

SCIENCE **From Seeds to Plants**

Contents

Contents

8

Acknowledgments

All photography © Pearson Education, Inc. (PEI) unless otherwise specifically noted.

Cover: © Gary Hubbell/Index Stock Imagery/PictureQuest.
3: © ThinkStock/SuperStock, Inc. 4: © Ariel Skelley/Corbis.
5: Myrleen Ferguson Cate/PhotoEdit. 6: © Morton Beebe/Corbis.
7: © James A. Sugar/Corbis. 8: Rick Stewart/Allsport/Getty Images, Inc. 10: © ThinkStock/SuperStock, Inc. 12: © Stephen Frisch/Stock Boston/PictureQuest. 14: Richard Hutchings/PhotoEdit. 16: Paul Bricknell/DK Images. 18: Daniel Bosler/Stone Allstock/Getty Images, Inc. 24: © Jonathan Nourok/PhotoEdit. 26: AP/Wide World Photo. 28: © Chuck Savage/Corbis. 30: Lawrence Migdale Photography. 32: © Ariel Skelley/Corbis. 38: C.C. Lockwood/Animals Animals/Earth Scenes. 40: Myrleen Ferguson Cate/PhotoEdit. 42: Peter Gardner/DK Images. 44: Kim Taylor and Jane Burton/DK Images. 46: Dick Luria/Taxi/Getty Images, Inc. 52: David Young-Wolff/PhotoEdit. 54: © Dana White/PhotoEdit. 56: Tony Freeman/PhotoEdit /PictureQuest. 58: © Morton Beebe/Corbis. 60: AP/Wide World Photo. 66: Demetrio Carrasco/DK Images. 68: EyeWire Collection/Getty Images, Inc. 70: © James A. Sugar/Corbis. 72: Mark Segal/Index Stock Imagery, Inc. 74: Bonnie Kamin/PhotoEdit. 80: The Granger Collection. 82: R.Y. Young/Library of Congress. 84: Rick Stewart/Allsport/ Getty Images, Inc. 86: © Bettmann/Corbis. 88: The Granger Collection.

Pets

Cats make good pets because
they like to live with people.

Pets and People

Pets are animals that live with people. Some animals, like lions, should never be pets because they are wild. However, many animals[25] can live with people. Some people keep fish to watch them swim. Others keep birds to hear them sing. Many people get pets to play[50] with, like dogs and cats.

All animals, even lions that live in the wild, need food, water, and places to move around and sleep. Pets[75] need owners who will give them these things.[83]

Pets

Hamsters are good pets because
they can be alone all day.

Kinds of Pets

Before they pick a pet, people need to know two things. They need to know what they want and what the pet[25] needs. If people want pets that can be alone all day, fish or hamsters are better pets than dogs. If people want pets that will[50] lie near them, cats are better pets than fish or hamsters.

To learn about pets, people need to read books and talk to pet owners.[75] Then both people and pets will be happy.[83]

Pets

Animal shelters have lots of dogs and other pets that need homes.

Where to Get Pets

If people want to have fish, birds, or hamsters as pets, they can find these animals in pet stores. Pets can[25] come from places other than stores, too.

Pet owners may give away or sell some of the babies their pets have. Animal shelters also sell[50] cats, dogs, and other pets. Animal shelters are places where animals stay if they do not have a home. Pets need many things, but the[75] thing they need most is a good home.[83]

A cage helps a pet bird stay safe.

Care of Pets

All animals need food, water, and safe places to move and sleep. Some pets have other needs, too. Birds need a pole[25] or bar to sit on. Hamsters need a wheel to run on. Fish need tanks with clean water. Dogs need places to run.

Different animals[50] need different kinds of food. Birds eat seeds. Dogs and cats eat meat. Hamsters need food that they can chew. Chewing keeps hamsters' teeth from[75] growing too big and hurting them.[81]

Pets

Pets and people need to know how
to be safe and happy together.

Fun With Pets

Owners need to teach their pets what the pets may do. People don't want their pets to be hurt. They also don't[25] want to be hurt by their pets.

Dogs need to learn when they may jump. They may jump for a ball, but they may not[50] jump on people. Cats with claws need a place to scratch. Without it, they may scratch a chair. When people teach their pets what the[75] pets may do, they and their pets are happy.[84]

 **Pets**

Write words that will help you remember what you learned.

Pets and People

_____

_____

_____

_____

Kinds of Pets

_____

_____

_____

_____

Where to Get Pets

_____

_____

_____

_____

Care of Pets

_____

_____

_____

_____

Fun With Pets

_____

_____

_____

_____

Pets and People

1. A pet is an animal ___

  Ⓐ that lives in a zoo.

  Ⓑ that is wild.

  Ⓒ that lives with people.

2. What are two things pets need?

_____

_____

_____

Kinds of Pets

1. Another good name for "Kinds of Pets" is ___

  Ⓐ "Picking a Pet."

  Ⓑ "Getting a Dog."

  Ⓒ "What Hamsters Need."

2. In what two ways can people learn about pets?

_____

_____

_____

 **Pets**

Where to Get Pets

1. An animal shelter is a place where animals stay if they ___

   Ⓐ need to find other animals.

   Ⓑ do not have a home.

   Ⓒ want to find owners.

2. Name two places you can get pets.

   _____

   _____

   _____

Care of Pets

1. "Care of Pets" is MAINLY about ___

   Ⓐ how people take care of pets.

   Ⓑ people who help pets.

   Ⓒ what pets eat.

2. Name the foods that two different pets eat.

   _____

   _____

   _____

Fun With Pets

1. What is the main idea of this reading?

   Ⓐ People should teach their pets.

   Ⓑ Pets can scratch.

   Ⓒ Pets are fun to play with.

2. Why should people teach their pets what to do?

_____

_____

_____

Connect Your Ideas

1. Name two ways people can make their pets happy.

_____

_____

_____

2. Suppose there was another reading. Do you think it would be about dogs or about lions? Why?

_____

_____

_____

Your Five Senses

How are these people using
their senses to stay safe?

What Is Happening?

A car honks its horn. A rainbow fills the sky. People know that these things are happening because of their five senses.[25] Their five senses help people see, hear, smell, taste, or touch the things around them.

With their sense of sight, people see the beautiful colors[50] in a rainbow. With their sense of hearing, people know that a car is coming down the street. Their five senses help people stay safe[75] and enjoy beautiful things around them.[81]

People who cannot see sometimes have
dogs that help them stay safe.

What Do You See?

Many people use their sense of sight more than any of their other five senses. Their sense of sight helps people[25] find safe places to walk. Their sense of sight also helps people enjoy beautiful things, like a picture. Most people see color, things that are[50] far away or near, and things that move.

Many people need glasses to see better. People who cannot see use their other senses, a cane,[75] or a dog to move around and stay safe.[84]

Your Five Senses

Hearing a funny story can make people smile.

What Do You Hear?

People also use their sense of hearing to know what is happening around them. A horn tells people to move out[25] of the way. A cry means that someone needs help.

There are many sounds that people enjoy hearing. A bird's song tells people that spring[50] is coming. A funny story makes people smile.

Some people need hearing aids to help them hear the sounds around them. People who cannot hear[75] use their other senses to stay safe.[82]

Your Five Senses

Their sense of smell can help people know
when something is good to eat.

What Do You Smell or Taste?

The smell of food cooking can make people's mouths water. That's because the senses of smell and taste often[25] work together. People don't want to taste food that smells bad. Food that smells bad can sometimes make people sick.

These two senses also work[50] by themselves. The smell of smoke warns that a fire has started. If people taste a food that is not good to eat, their sense[75] of taste can make them spit it out.[83]

Their sense of touch tells people
that snow is cold.

What Do You Feel?

The sense of touch is very important when people can't find out what's happening with their other senses. Their sense of[25] touch helps people get around in the dark. They can even use it to find a light switch.

Their sense of touch tells people when[50] something is too hot or cold to hold. Their sense of touch also tells people how hard to move a pen. Babies use their sense[75] of touch to learn about the world.[82]

Write words that will help you remember what you learned.

What Is Happening?

_____

_____

_____

_____

What Do You See?

_____

_____

_____

_____

What Do You Hear?

_____

_____

_____

_____

What Do You Smell or Taste?

_____

_____

_____

_____

What Do You Feel?

_____

_____

_____

_____

What Is Happening?

1. Another good name for "What Is Happening?" is ___

(A) "See and Smell."

(B) "The Five Senses."

(C) "Seeing Rainbows."

2. What do people's senses help them do?

_____

_____

_____

What Do You See?

1. This reading is MAINLY about ___

(A) how people use their sight.

(B) the colors in the rainbow.

(C) how to use glasses.

2. What are two ways people use their sight?

_____

_____

_____

What Do You Hear?

1. People can use their hearing ___

   Ⓐ to pick food.

   Ⓑ to enjoy sounds.

   Ⓒ to find a rainbow.

2. What are two ways hearing can help people?

_____

_____

_____

What Do You Smell or Taste?

1. Which sense can warn that a fire has started?

   Ⓐ smell

   Ⓑ taste

   Ⓒ smoke

2. How can smell and taste keep people safe?

_____

_____

_____

What Do You Feel?

1. Their sense of touch helps people ___

Ⓐ taste their food.

Ⓑ get around in the dark.

Ⓒ know if a car is coming.

2. Name three things you can learn by touching something.

_____

_____

_____

Connect Your Ideas

1. How do you use your senses when you eat dinner?

_____

_____

_____

2. How could you use your senses of sight and hearing together?

_____

_____

_____

From Seeds to Plants

This coconut seed is starting to
grow into a coconut tree.

Seeds

How are beans, rice, and coconuts the same? They all are kinds of seeds. A seed is where most plants begin life. There are[25] other ways plants can begin life, but most plants begin as seeds.

Seeds come in lots of different shapes and colors. Some are small and[50] light, like rose seeds and apple seeds. Others are large and heavy. The largest seed in the world is the coconut. The coconut has a[75] hard shell and is very heavy.[81]

From Seeds to Plants

Pumpkins are much bigger than pumpkin seeds.

How Seeds Look

Most seeds don't look like the plants they become. A white pumpkin seed does not have the color or shape of a[25] pumpkin. However, a pumpkin seed will only become a pumpkin.

The size of seeds also does not match the size of the plants they become.[50] Apple seeds are smaller than pumpkin seeds. However, the apple tree that grows from an apple seed is much bigger than the pumpkin plant that[75] grows from a pumpkin seed.[80]

From Seeds to Plants

This baby bean plant is pushing through
its seed as it starts to grow.

Parts of a Seed

Seeds have three parts. One part is the seed coat that keeps the inside of the seed safe. Inside the seed[25] are two parts: the baby plant and food it uses to grow.

To see inside a seed, put beans in water for a day. The[50] water makes the seed coat soft. Soon, the baby plant pushes through the soft seed coat. The baby plant uses the food inside the seed[75] until the plant can make its own food.[83]

From Seeds to Plants

This picture shows a baby bean plant's root, stem, and leaves.

Seeds to Plants

Once the coat of a seed gets soft, the baby plant can push through and begin to grow. A stem and roots[25] soon form. The stem grows toward the Sun. The Sun's rays give the plant some of the things it needs to make its own food.[50]

The plant's roots grow down into the earth. The roots get water and other things from the earth into the plant. Now the plant can[75] grow as it makes its own food.[82]

From Seeds to Plants

The wheat that grows from seeds is used
to make many kinds of bread.

The Importance of Seeds

Without seeds, few new plants would grow. If there were no plants, people and animals would not have the food they[25] need. Without plants, the air that people and animals need would not have the right mix.

Many people and animals also eat different kinds of[50] seeds. People around the world eat many kinds of seeds every day. Some of the seeds people eat are rice, oats, wheat, and beans. Plants[75] and seeds help people in many ways.[82]

REVIEW From Seeds to Plants

Write words that will help you remember what you learned.

Seeds

_____

_____

_____

_____

How Seeds Look

_____

_____

_____

_____

Parts of a Seed

_____

_____

_____

_____

Seeds to Plants

_____

_____

_____

_____

The Importance of Seeds

_____

_____

_____

_____

Seeds

1. How are beans, rice, and coconuts the same?

   Ⓐ They are all seeds.

   Ⓑ They all grow on trees.

   Ⓒ They are all the same color.

2. Tell what you learned about seeds.

_____

_____

_____

How Seeds Look

1. Which of these sentences is true?

   Ⓐ Most seeds do not look like the plants they become.

   Ⓑ Seeds are the same size as the plants they become.

   Ⓒ Small seeds always become small plants.

2. How are apple seeds and pumpkin seeds different?

_____

_____

_____

From Seeds to Plants

Parts of a Seed

1. What is the main idea of this reading?

Ⓐ Seeds make their own food.

Ⓑ Seeds have three parts.

Ⓒ Seeds need water.

2. How do plants start to grow from seeds?

_____

_____

_____

Seeds to Plants

1. Another good name for "Seeds to Plants" is ___

Ⓐ "Food From the Sun."

Ⓑ "Inside a Seed."

Ⓒ "How Seeds Grow."

2. Tell how plants grow from seeds.

_____

_____

_____

The Importance of Seeds

1. Seeds are important because they ___

   Ⓐ save water.

   Ⓑ make plants.

   Ⓒ feed plants.

2. Tell about two ways plants help people.

_____

_____

_____

Connect Your Ideas

1. What are two things you learned about seeds?

_____

_____

_____

2. Name three kinds of seeds and plants you use.

_____

_____

_____

Every country has its own flag.

Our Country

It is likely that you live in the United States of America. The United States of America is also called "the United States"[25] or "the U.S." People who live in the United States are called "Americans."

The United States is one of the 193 countries in the world.[50] A country is an area of land. In this area of land, everyone has the same government. A government is made up of the leaders[75] who make the rules for that country's people.[83]

Even students in the United States
have "rule by the people."

Rule by the People

The United States government is ruled by the people. "Rule by the people" means that Americans vote for their government's leaders.[25] The leaders did not take over the country with an army. The leaders are also not kings or queens who can rule forever.

"Rule by[50] the people" does not mean that people can do anything they want. It means that those who get the most votes make the rules. Voters[75] can pick new leaders every few years.[82]

One right Americans have
is the right to vote.

Rules and Rights

Everyone in the United States must follow the country's rules. For example, everyone must pay taxes on what they earn.

The American[25] way of life, however, is not just about rules. Americans have many rights, too. They can vote for their leaders. People also have the right[50] to be treated in a fair way, no matter who they are. Some laws give rights that were important long ago. For example, Americans don't[75] have to let the army live in their home.[84]

The United States of America

People come to live in the United States
from countries all around the world.

People From Many Places

Most of the people who live in Mexico were born there. Most of the people in Mexico have parents who were[25] born there, too. Many people who live in the United States, however, were born in another country. Many people also have parents who were born[50] in another country.

For many years, people came to the United States to be able to vote. Today, people in many countries can vote. Still,[75] many people come to live in the United States.[84]

Today, the United States has both women
and African American leaders.

Freedom for All

America's first leaders had the idea that everyone would be free and could vote. However, their idea meant that only people who[25] looked like the leaders were free and could vote. No leaders were women. It took almost 150 years before women could vote.

No leaders were[50] African American either. For almost the first 100 years of the new country, many African Americans were slaves. Today, all Americans can vote. Today, the[75] idea "freedom for all" means "freedom for all people."[84]

The United States of America

Write words that will help you remember what you learned.

Our Country

_____

_____

_____

_____

Rule by the People

_____

_____

_____

_____

Rules and Rights

_____

_____

_____

_____

People From Many Places

_____

_____

_____

_____

Freedom for All

_____

_____

_____

_____

Our Country

1. Another good name for "Our Country" is ___

   Ⓐ "The United States."

   Ⓑ "Governments of the World."

   Ⓒ "Different Countries."

2. What do the leaders in a government do?

_____

_____

_____

Rule by the People

1. All Americans can vote ___

   Ⓐ for kings.

   Ⓑ for the army.

   Ⓒ for their leaders.

2. What does "rule by the people" mean?

_____

_____

_____

The United States of America

Rules and Rights

1. What is the main idea of this reading?

   Ⓐ Americans can vote.

   Ⓑ Americans pay taxes.

   Ⓒ Americans have rules and rights.

2. Tell about one right Americans have.

_____

_____

_____

People From Many Places

1. This reading is MAINLY about ___

   Ⓐ how many people live in the United States.

   Ⓑ why people in other countries can vote.

   Ⓒ where people were born who live in the United States.

2. What is one way many countries are like the United States today?

_____

_____

_____

Freedom for All

1. What is the main idea of this reading?

   Ⓐ No American leaders are women.

   Ⓑ All Americans are free today.

   Ⓒ Only American leaders are free.

2. What does "freedom for all" mean today?

   _____

   _____

   _____

Connect Your Ideas

1. What are two things you learned about the United States government?

   _____

   _____

   _____

2. Suppose there was another reading. Would it be about one of the states or about another country? Why?

   _____

   _____

   _____

American Places

Some of the special places
in America are parks.

Special Places

Many people have places that are special to them. Children have special places to play. Families have special places to eat.

Our country,[25] America, has special places, too. Some special American places are parks. People visit these parks to see trees or animals that are not found anywhere[50] else. Other American places are special because important things took place there. All of these places must be used with care so that people will[75] be able to visit them years from now.[83]

American Places

The White House is the place where the President
of the United States lives and works.

The White House

The President of the United States lives and works in the White House. This place wasn't always called the White House, though.[25] In fact, it wasn't even painted white until 1810. That was when it got its name.

To keep the president and others safe, not as[50] many people can visit the White House today as in the past. However, the White House is still the only president's house in the world[75] that people can visit for free.[81]

Some national parks have swamps
that people can visit and study.

The National Park Service

Most people think of parks as places with trees and grass. Parks have other things, too. The National Park Service takes[25] care of special parks in America. Some national parks have trees and grass. Some national parks also have caves, swamps, and sand dunes.

Besides parks,[50] the National Park Service takes care of places and things that were important in America's past, like ships, trains, and even schools. Every state has[75] places that are special to America.[81]

American Places

The Library of Congress is the largest
library in the world today.

The Library of Congress

The nation's library is called the Library of Congress. It began in 1800 with 152 books. Today, though, the Library of [25] Congress is the world's largest library. It has more than 100,000,000 books, maps, tapes, pictures, and other things.

People don't have to visit the Library [50] of Congress to use it. They can use a computer to see things in the Library of Congress. A computer can show people some of [75] the books, maps, and pictures in our nation's library. [84]

American Places

The U.S. Postal Service picks up mail and
brings it to people's homes.

The U.S. Postal Service

You may never go to some of the places that Americans share because they are far from your home. However, one[25] place that Americans share is close to where most people live. It's the U.S. Postal Service.

Most days, someone from the U.S. Postal Service brings[50] mail to mailboxes at people's homes. These mailboxes are small parts of the U.S. Postal Service. Even though they are very small, mailboxes are places[75] that everyone in America shares.[80]

REVIEW American Places

Write words that will help you remember what you learned.

Special Places

_____

_____

_____

_____

The White House

_____

_____

_____

_____

The National Park Service

_____

_____

_____

_____

The Library of Congress

_____

_____

_____

_____

The U.S. Postal Service

_____

_____

_____

_____

Special Places

1. "Special Places" is MAINLY about ___

   Ⓐ our homes and parks.

   Ⓑ places children play.

   Ⓒ places that are important.

2. Tell about why some parks are special to America.

   _____

   _____

   _____

The White House

1. Where does the President of the United States live and work?

   Ⓐ in the states

   Ⓑ in the White House

   Ⓒ in the parks

2. How is the White House different from other presidents' houses?

   _____

   _____

   _____

American Places

The National Park Service

1. Besides trees and grass, some national parks have ___

   Ⓐ places where people live.

   Ⓑ the White Houses of other leaders.

   Ⓒ caves, swamps, and sand dunes.

2. What two things does the National Park Service take care of?

_____

_____

_____

The Library of Congress

1. Another good name for "The Library of Congress" is ___

   Ⓐ "Books and Maps."

   Ⓑ "America's Library."

   Ⓒ "Computers in the Library."

2. Name three things that are in the Library of Congress.

_____

_____

_____

The U.S. Postal Service

1. Which of these is a place Americans share?

Ⓐ their homes

Ⓑ their mail

Ⓒ the U.S. Postal Service

2. What does the U.S. Postal Service do?

_____

_____

_____

Connect Your Ideas

1. How are the White House, the Library of Congress, and the U.S. Postal Service alike?

_____

_____

_____

2. Which of these American places would you like to visit? Why?

_____

_____

_____

Sarah Hale worked to make Thanksgiving a national holiday.

Sarah Hale

When Sarah Hale was a child more than 200 years ago, Thanksgiving was not a national holiday in the United States. At that[25] time, most women did not have jobs. Sarah Hale was one woman who did have a job. She was a writer.

Sarah Hale believed that[50] Thanksgiving was an important day. She believed that it should be a national holiday. For 26 years, Sarah Hale wrote and spoke about this dream.[75] At last, in 1867, Thanksgiving became a national holiday.[84]

President Teddy Roosevelt worked to make
sure all people could enjoy nature.

Teddy Roosevelt

President Teddy Roosevelt believed that nature was an important part of the United States. He believed that people should care for the animals,[25] plants, trees, and land in nature. President Roosevelt's dream was that nature would always be there to enjoy.

As President of the United States, Teddy[50] Roosevelt worked for laws to make this happen. These laws gave the United States parks that millions of people enjoy each year. Because Teddy Roosevelt[75] loved animals, people call stuffed toy bears "teddy bears."[84]

Kristi Yamaguchi won an Olympic gold medal as the best woman ice skater in the world.

Kristi Yamaguchi

As a child, Kristi Yamaguchi dreamed about being an ice skater in the Olympic Games. When she was born, one of Kristi's feet[25] had a problem. This meant that she had to work even harder to become an Olympic ice skater. Kristi's family helped her work to make[50] her dream come true.

In 1992, Kristi Yamaguchi won the Olympic gold medal as the best woman ice skater in the world. Kristi says, "Just[75] do your very best, and always dream."[82]

Americans Who Dream

Wilbur and Orville Wright made the
first airplane that could fly.

The Wright Brothers

When they were children, Wilbur and Orville Wright flew kites. At that time, there were no airplanes. However, Wilbur and Orville dreamed[25] about flying through the air.

After they grew up, the Wright brothers began making an airplane. They faced many problems. At last, though, they made[50] an airplane that could fly. Their airplane flew for only 59 seconds, but the Wright brothers were still the first people to fly. The Wright[75] brothers' dream led to the airplanes of today.[83]

Charles Drew found a way to keep blood fresh
and save many people's lives.

Charles Drew

When Charles Drew was young, it was hard for African Americans to become doctors. Charles Drew, who was African American, did not let[25] that stop him. He worked hard, and he finally became a doctor.

Charles Drew also worked hard to find the answer to an important problem.[50] He found a way to keep blood fresh. When blood can be kept fresh, it can be used to make people well. Because of Charles[75] Drew's dream, millions of lives are saved every year.[84]

Write words that will help you remember what you learned.

Sarah Hale

_____

_____

_____

_____

Teddy Roosevelt

_____

_____

_____

_____

Kristi Yamaguchi

_____

_____

_____

_____

The Wright Brothers

_____

_____

_____

_____

Charles Drew

_____

_____

_____

_____

Sarah Hale

1. The main idea of this reading is that ___

Ⓐ women have jobs now.

Ⓑ Sarah Hale wanted a holiday.

Ⓒ all countries should have holidays.

2. What was Sarah Hale's dream?

_____

_____

_____

Teddy Roosevelt

1. President Roosevelt worked for laws that ___

Ⓐ made teddy bears.

Ⓑ made nature.

Ⓒ made parks.

2. What was President Teddy Roosevelt's dream?

_____

_____

_____

Americans Who Dream

Kristi Yamaguchi

1. Another good name for "Kristi Yamaguchi" is ___

   Ⓐ "The Olympic Games."

   Ⓑ "A Skater's Dream."

   Ⓒ "How to Ice Skate."

2. What was Kristi Yamaguchi's dream?

   _____

   _____

   _____

The Wright Brothers

1. After they grew up, the Wright brothers ___

   Ⓐ made an airplane.

   Ⓑ flew kites.

   Ⓒ made today's airplanes.

2. What was the Wright brothers' dream?

   _____

   _____

   _____

Charles Drew

1. Charles Drew's dream was to become ___

   Ⓐ a doctor.

   Ⓑ a teacher.

   Ⓒ a writer.

2. What did Charles Drew find a way to do?

_____

_____

_____

Connect Your Ideas

1. How did two of these people make their dream come true?

_____

_____

_____

2. Tell about one way all of these people are alike.

_____

_____

_____

Reading Log · Level A · Book 1

	I Read This	New Words I Learned	New Facts I Learned	What Else I Want to Learn About This Subject
Pets				
Pets and People				
Kinds of Pets				
Where to Get Pets				
Care of Pets				
Fun With Pets				
Your Five Senses				
What Is Happening?				
What Do You See?				
What Do You Hear?				
What Do You Smell or Taste?				
What Do You Feel?				
From Seeds to Plants				
Seeds				
How Seeds Look				
Parts of a Seed				
Seeds to Plants				
The Importance of Seeds				

Reading Log • Level A • Book 1

	I Read This	New Words I Learned	New Facts I Learned	What Else I Want to Learn About This Subject
The United States of America				
Our Country				
Rule by the People				
Rules and Rights				
People From Many Places				
Freedom for All				
American Places				
Special Places				
The White House				
The National Park Service				
The Library of Congress				
The U.S. Postal Service				
Americans Who Dream				
Sarah Hale				
Teddy Roosevelt				
Kristi Yamaguchi				
The Wright Brothers				
Charles Drew				

Self-Check Graph

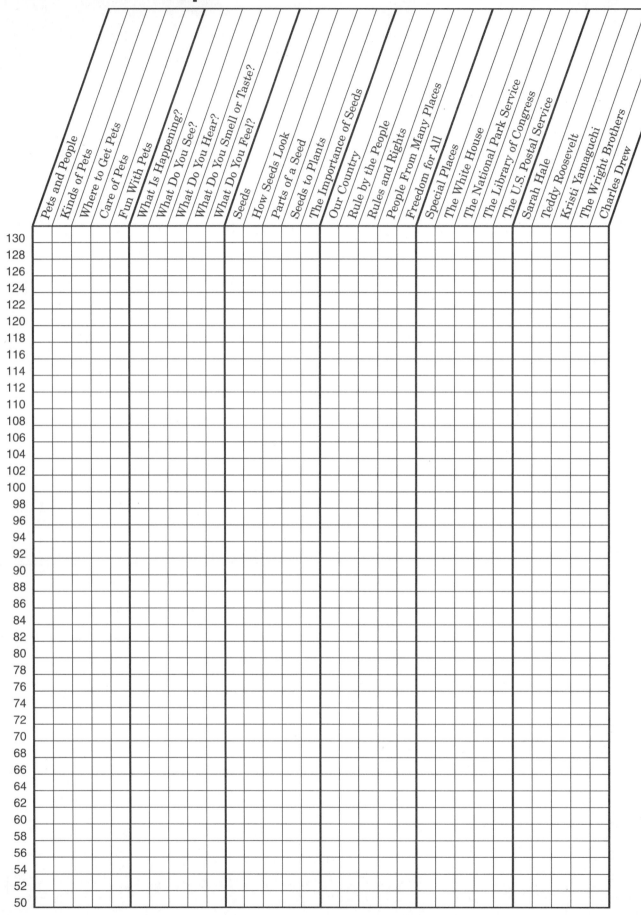

Mark your reading rate here.

	Pets and People	Kinds of Pets	Where to Get Pets	Care of Pets	Fun With Pets	What Is Happening?	What Do You See?	What Do You Hear?	What Do You Smell or Taste?	What Do You Feel?	Seeds	How Seeds Look	Parts of a Seed	Seeds to Plants	The Importance of Seeds	Our Country	Rule by the People	Rules and Rights	People From Many Places	Freedom for All	Special Places	The White House	The National Park Service	The Library of Congress	The U.S. Postal Service	Sarah Hale	Teddy Roosevelt	Kristi Yamaguchi	The Wright Brothers	Charles Drew
130																														
128																														
126																														
124																														
122																														
120																														
118																														
116																														
114																														
112																														
110																														
108																														
106																														
104																														
102																														
100																														
98																														
96																														
94																														
92																														
90																														
88																														
86																														
84																														
82																														
80																														
78																														
76																														
74																														
72																														
70																														
68																														
66																														
64																														
62																														
60																														
58																														
56																														
54																														
52																														
50																														